Animal Neighbours

Bat

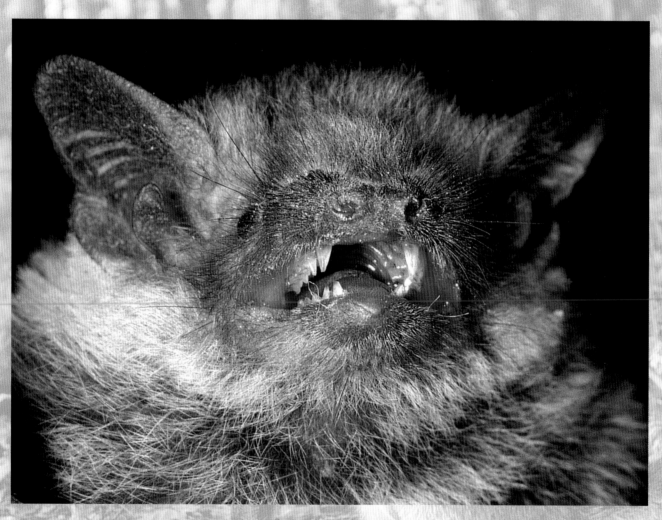

Stephen Savage

WAYLAND

Animal Neighbours

Titles in this series:

Badger • Bat • Deer • Fox • Hare • Hedgehog
Mole • Mouse • Otter • Owl • Rat • Swallow

Conceived and produced for Hodder Wayland by

Nutshell
MEDIA

Intergen House, 65–67 Westerm Road, Hove BN3 2JQ UK
www.nutshellmedialtd.co.uk

Commission Editor: Vicky Brooker
Designer: Tim Mayer
Illustrator: Jackie Harland
Picture Research: Glass Onion Pictures

Published in Great Britain in 2004 by Hodder Wayland, an imprint of Hodder Children's Books.

This paperback edition published in 2007 by Wayland, an imprint of Hachette Children's Books.

British Library Cataloguing in Publication Data
Savage, Stephen, 1965–
Bat. – (Animal neighbours)
1. Bats – Juvenile literature
I. Title
599.4

ISBN-13: 978 0 7502 5079 5

Cover: A pipistrelle bat chases its insect prey in mid-air.
Title pages: A close-up photograph showing the bat's small, sharp teeth.

Picture acknowledgements
FLPA *Title page* (B. Borrell), 8 (H. Clark), 11 (Hugh Clark), 21 (B. Borrell), 25 (H. Clark), 26 (Peter Dean), 28 top (H. Clark), 28 bottom (Hugh Clark); naturepl.com 7 (Jim Clare), 10 (Dietmar Nill), 12 (Hans Christoph Kappel), 14 (Dietmar Nill), 22 (Steve Packham), 28 left (Dietmar Nill); NHPA *Cover* (Stephen Dalton), 9 (Melvin Grey), 13, 20 (Stephen Dalton), 28 right (Melvin Grey); OSF 6 (Partridge Films Ltd), 19 (Richard Packwood), 23 (Carlos Sanchez Alonso), 27 (Alastair Shay); rspb-images.com 24 (Gerald Downey); RSPCA Photolibrary 16–17 (Duncan McEwan).

Colour reproductions by Dot Gradations Ltd, UK
Printed and bound in China.

Wayland,
an imprint of Hachette Children's Books
338 Euston Road, London NW1 3BH

Contents

Meet the Bat

Bats are small, flying mammals, with furry bodies and leathery wings. There are about 925 species alive today, living mainly in old trees, caves and buildings. They are found almost everywhere in the world except the polar regions and very hot deserts.

This book is about the pipistrelle bat, which is the smallest European bat.

▲ The red shading on this map shows where the pipistrelle bat lives in the world today.

Thumb

The thumb has a claw that is used for grooming, crawling, climbing and sometimes handling food.

BAT FACTS

The pipistrelle bat's scientific name is *Pipistrellus pipistrellus*, which comes from the Latin word meaning 'bat'.

In ancient English, the pipistrelle bat was known as 'flittermouse', because of its jerky flight.

Pipistrelle bats have an average head and body length of 3.5–4.5 cm and a wingspan of 19–25 cm. However, when its wings are folded back, the pipistrelle can fit inside a matchbox.

Pipistrelle bats weigh between 3–8 g, although the average weight is 5 g. This is lighter than a 2p coin.

▲ This shows the size of the pipistrelle bat compared to an adult human hand.

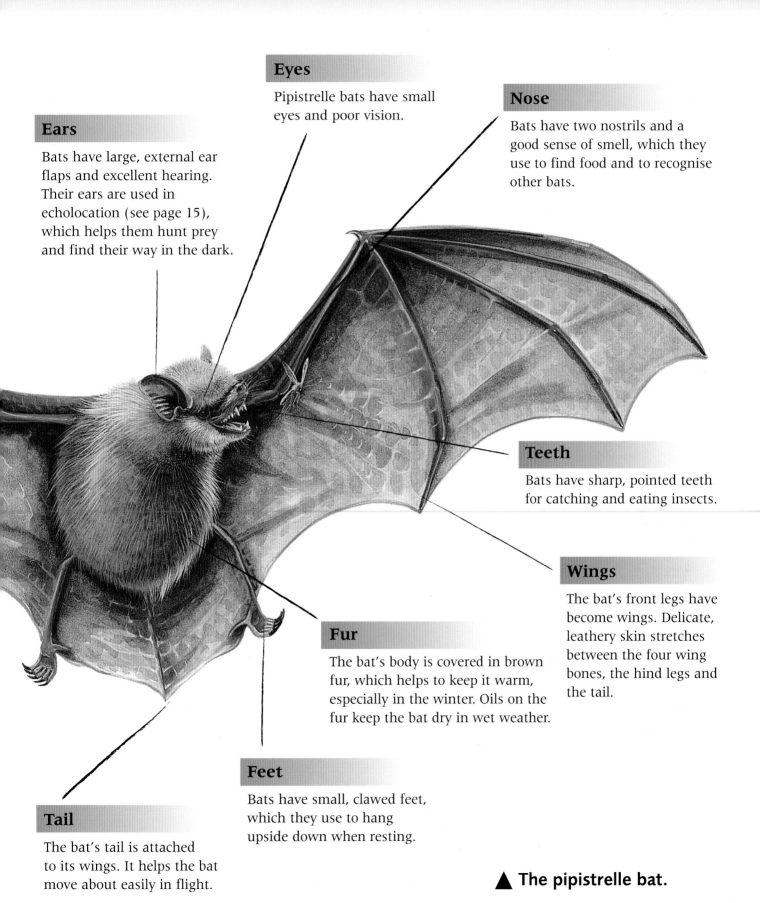

Eyes

Pipistrelle bats have small eyes and poor vision.

Nose

Bats have two nostrils and a good sense of smell, which they use to find food and to recognise other bats.

Ears

Bats have large, external ear flaps and excellent hearing. Their ears are used in echolocation (see page 15), which helps them hunt prey and find their way in the dark.

Teeth

Bats have sharp, pointed teeth for catching and eating insects.

Wings

The bat's front legs have become wings. Delicate, leathery skin stretches between the four wing bones, the hind legs and the tail.

Fur

The bat's body is covered in brown fur, which helps to keep it warm, especially in the winter. Oils on the fur keep the bat dry in wet weather.

Feet

Bats have small, clawed feet, which they use to hang upside down when resting.

Tail

The bat's tail is attached to its wings. It helps the bat move about easily in flight.

▲ **The pipistrelle bat.**

The Bat Family

Bats belong to a group of mammals called Chiroptera, which means 'hand wing'. Scientists have divided this group into smaller groups, known as families, containing bat species that have similar features.

Most bats are insectivores, eating mainly insects, but some species eat very different food. The Indian flying fox lives in the tropical forests of southern Asia. It is one of the largest bats in the world and eats only fruit. The Mexican fishing bat of South America lives on small islands near marine lagoons. It plucks fish from the water using its feet.

▲ Fruit bats, like this Peter's epauletted fruit bat, use sight and smell to find fruit.

BIGGEST AND SMALLEST

The largest bats are the fruit bats (also known as flying foxes), which are found in Australia, Asia and Africa. Fruit bats have a wingspan of over 1.5 m. The smallest bat is the bumblebee bat from Thailand, which has a wingspan of 15 cm.

As well as insects, the Australian ghost bat eats reptiles, frogs, birds, small mammals, and even other bat species. It kills its prey by wrapping its wings around the victim and giving a deathly bite to the neck.

Vampire bats from South America have the most unusual diet of all bats. They feed only on the blood of other animals. They will attack domestic and other animals, but they do not attack people.

▼ A vampire bat laps up blood with its tongue. The bat's saliva stops the blood from clotting.

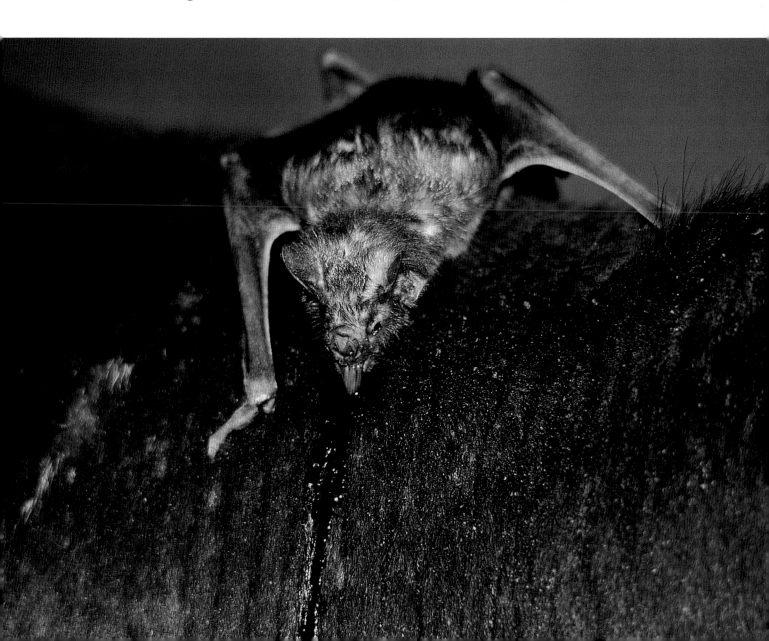

Birth and Growing Up

It is summertime, and a female pipistrelle bat prepares to give birth. This may be in a hole in a wall or roof, in a tree, or behind some vegetation. The female usually shares this nursery roost with many other female bats that are also pregnant (see box on page 11). She gives birth to a single, tiny, furless pup, born with its eyes and ears tightly shut.

At night, the female bat leaves her pup in the nursery roost while she joins the other females to catch and eat insects. When left alone, the young furless bats huddle together for warmth. The warmer the pups are, the quicker they will grow.

BAT PUPS

Young bats are called pups. Most pups are born between June and mid-July.

Most bats give birth to a single pup, although twins may be born on rare occasions.

New-born pipistrelle bats are about 2 cm long and weigh about 1.3 g.

▼ This bat pup (on the left) is just 4 days old.

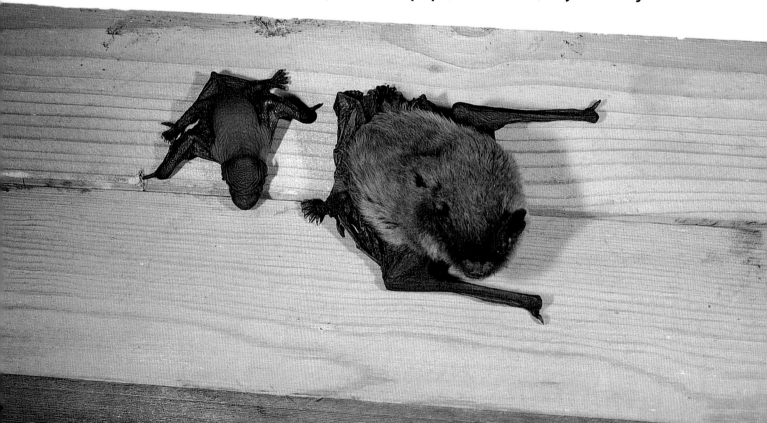

▲ A female bat allows her pup to suckle from teats underneath her body.

The female bats return several times in the night to suckle their pups with milk. When they return to the nursery the pups call out. Each female recognises her own pup by its call, and then, when she gets closer, by its scent. During the day, the females stay inside the nursery roost, feeding their pups and sleeping.

▲ A female bat and two pups look out from the entrance of their nursery roost.

Early days

When it is about 1 week old, the pup's eyes open. It grows quickly and by 3 weeks old, it is covered in fur. Now the pup is ready to leave the nursery roost for its first flight.

Many of the other female bats will also have young of about the same age. At dusk, the mother and pup join the other female bats and their young as they fly about near the entrance to the nursery roost. This is a difficult time for young bats. At first they do not fly well and many fall to the ground, where they can be reached by predators such as cats.

Once it can fly, after the age of 3 weeks, the young bat soon learns to catch flying insects by following and copying the females. The mother continues to suckle her pup as it starts to eat solid food, but by the time it is 6 weeks old, the pup will be weaned and able to look after itself. It is now time for the females and young bats to leave the nursery roost and find other roost sites.

NURSERY ROOSTS

The average nursery roost contains between 50 and 100 female bats, each with a pup, although up to 1,000 bats may gather together. Female bats usually choose nursery sites that face south or south-west, to get most of the sun's heat. If the roost gets too hot or too cold, the mother may fly to another site. If the pup is too young to fly by this time, it can hang on to the underside of its mother using its clawed feet.

▼ This 5-week-old pup is eating mostly insect food and is almost weaned.

Habitat

Once the young bats have left the nursery roost for good, they will search for a new home. Pipistrelle bats live in a wide range of different habitats. In the countryside, they live in woodlands, wetlands and farmland. In towns and cities, they can be found in gardens and parks. They also live in houses and other buildings. Since bats need to drink water every night, they often live within 400 metres of a stream, river, pond or lake.

Most bats are nocturnal. They feed at night and rest during the day. Pipistrelle bats do not make a nest. Instead, they make their home in places that are well-hidden from predators, and sheltered from the extreme heat or cold. These places are known as roost sites.

◀ **Hanging upside down, this roosting bat clings to the bark of a tree with its strong clawed feet.**

▼ **This bat is leaving its roost site in a loft. The bat's ability to fly means that it can catch and eat animals that most other mammals cannot.**

Roost sites are often confined spaces, such as between roof felt or tiles, or behind tree bark, where the bats sleep upright. The entrance to the roost can be a hole as small as 5 millimetres wide. In larger spaces, such as inside hollow trees, in lofts or in artificical bat boxes, bats hang upside down from their clawed feet.

Flying

Although some mammals can glide, bats are the only mammals that are capable of sustained flight. Like birds, bats have light bones. Their light weight reduces the energy bats need to stay in the air. However, flying still requires a lot of energy.

When they are ready to fly, bats that are resting by hanging upside down simply let go and open their wings. This is a good way of getting airborne without too much effort. The bat uses its chest and wing muscles to pull its wings down, pushing it forward through the air. Its back muscles are used to raise the wings. A pipistrelle bat's wings beat about 20 times a second, which keeps the bat moving forwards.

▲ The main reason to fly is to find food. A bat may forage up to 5 kilometres from its roost.

Echolocation

Although bats cannot see well in the dark, they navigate and find prey using echolocation. As they fly, bats make high-pitched sounds in their larynx (voice box), which are sent out through their mouth or nose. These sounds bounce off objects and moving prey in front of the bat, and the echoes are picked up by the bat's ears. The echoes form a 'sound picture' of the bat's surroundings in its brain.

▼ **This diagram shows how a bat finds prey using echolocation.**

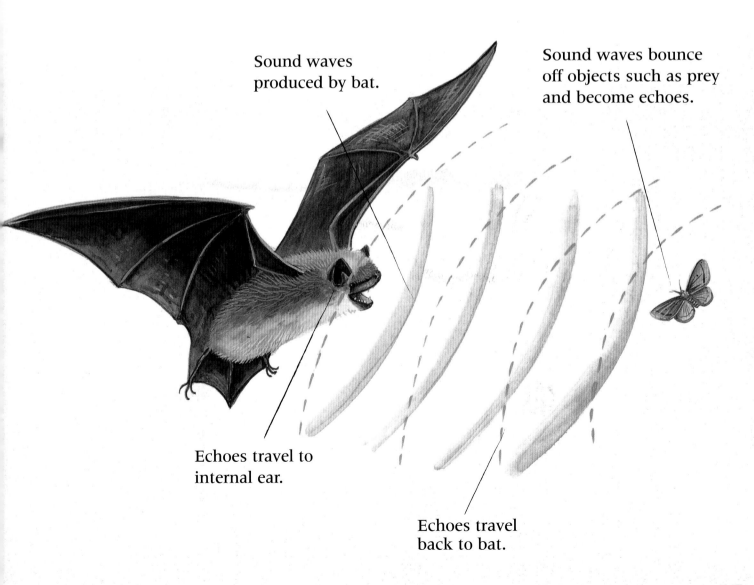

Sound waves produced by bat.

Sound waves bounce off objects such as prey and become echoes.

Echoes travel to internal ear.

Echoes travel back to bat.

Hibernation roosts

Every winter, when insect food becomes scarce and their food supply runs out, pipistrelle bats hibernate. During the autumn, they eat more insects than usual and store some of this food in their body as fat. When they have built up enough fat, the bats look for special roost sites, where they will hibernate through most of the winter.

Hibernation sites include houses and beneath the bark of old trees. Some pipistrelle bats hibernate alone, but most form colonies with as many as 60 or

HIBERNATION

When a bat hibernates, it enters a much deeper sleep than normal sleep. Its breathing and heart rate are much slower than usual, and its body temperature drops. This type of sleep uses up less energy than normal sleep, which is important since the bat is not replacing energy with food.

▲ These pipistrelle bats are huddled together in their hibernation roost, in the roof space of a house.

even several hundred bats. Young bats often hibernate in the same roost as their mother, in mixed groups containing both male and female bats. The bats huddle together in the roost for warmth.

The sleeping bats live off their store of body fat during hibernation. When they start to hibernate, the bats may weigh as much as 8 grams, but after hibernation their weight may have dropped to as little as 3 grams. In warm winter weather, the bats sometimes wake from hibernation for a few days and hunt insects to build up their fat reserves. They will wake up properly in the warm months of spring.

Food

Pipistrelle bats are insectivores. They feed on a wide variety of small flying insects, including gnats, caddis flies, moths and mosquitoes. Each bat must eat about half its own body weight in insects a night to replace the energy used by flying.

▼ Bats eat many insects, but only a few predators eat bats. (The illustrations are not to scale.)

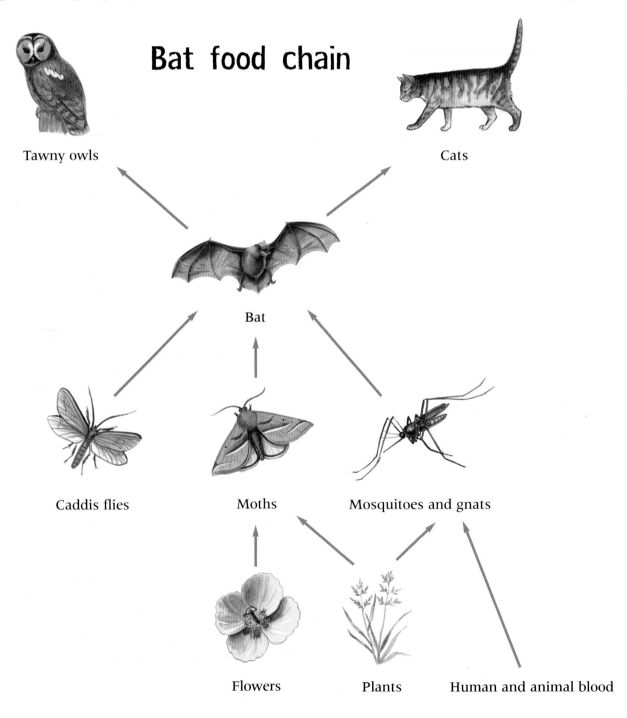

Bat food chain

Tawny owls

Cats

Bat

Caddis flies

Moths

Mosquitoes and gnats

Flowers

Plants

Human and animal blood

▲ When bats catch larger prey, such as this caddis fly, they may rest to eat. Smaller insects such as gnats are eaten in flight.

The bat's diet varies according to the type of insects that are most plentiful each night. The biggest swarms of flying insects are usually found on warm, still summer nights, since these conditions are easiest for flight.

Gardens are favourite feeding sites for pipistrelle bats. Flying insects, such as moths, are attracted to honeysuckle, evening primrose and other flowers that produce scent at night. Bats are often seen flying low over streams, ponds or lakes, where there is plenty of insect food as well as water for drinking. Bats drink while flying low and scoop up water with their lower jaw.

19

Hunting

Pipistrelle bats leave their daytime roost sites at dusk, just after sunset. Hungry after a day's rest, this is the time when bats are the most active. On warm evenings, when there is a lot of insect prey around, they may even emerge earlier than dusk.

▼ **This bat has spotted a caddis fly. Bats can eat as many as 20 insects a minute.**

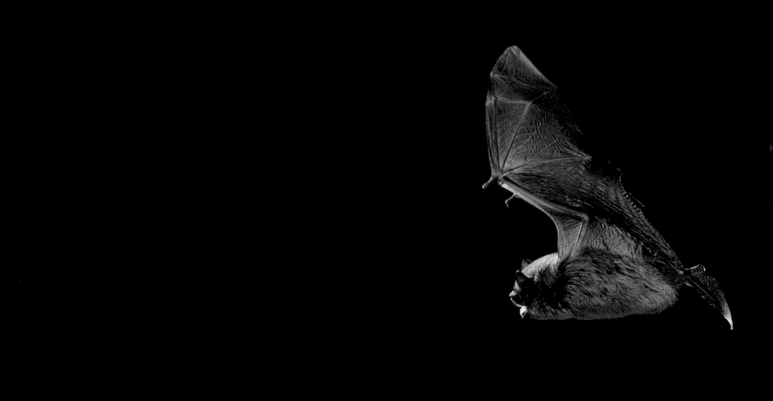

Bats hunt their prey in open spaces around buildings or trees, or above streams and lakes. They fly along hedges and tree lines to help find their way in the dark. Pipistrelle bats usually fly between 2–20 metres above the ground. They are very agile and snatch insects from the air in their mouths.

▲ The bat's tiny sharp teeth are perfect for chewing soft-bodied insects.

In its search for insects, a bat will patrol a wide area using echolocation (see page 15). If it can detect only a few insects, it will quickly move on to another area, returning again later. If there are lots of insects present, the bat may stay in the same area for over two hours. A bat will eat up to 3,000 insects in a single night.

TERRITORIAL

When insect food is in short supply, pipistrelle bats warn other bats to stay away by producing a high-pitched call. They do this to keep the little food that is available for themselves, becoming territorial over the area.

Bats do not hunt continually throughout each night. In between each hunting trip they will rest, either in a temporary roost site or by simply hanging upside down from a branch.

Finding a Mate

Pipistrelle bats mate at the beginning of winter. The males attract females by making soft chirps. The calls are repeated frequently as the males fly back and forth near their roost.

Once a male has attracted a female, he may defend her against other males. Each male bat will mate with more than one female.

After mating, the bats gather together in mixed colonies to hibernate. The females will not become pregnant until the spring, so that their young are born in the warm summer months and have a better chance of survival. This is called delayed implantation.

◀ **This male and female bat are roosting in the roof of a church.**

▲ There are hundreds of bats and their young in this nursery colony of Schreiber's bats, in Spain.

MATING

Female pipistrelle bats are ready to mate when they are a year old. Males are usually 2 years old before they can mate, possibly so they are big enough to compete with other males for females.

Female bats are pregnant for 44–50 days before giving birth. In some parts of the world, female pipistrelle bats often give birth to twins.

When the bats wake up from hibernation, the females leave the hibernation roost and form a maternity colony with other pregnant females. They huddle together for warmth in the nursery roost, saving energy for the growing pups inside them.

The males play no part in the rearing of their pups so they do not leave the hibernation roost with the females. But soon they leave and find summer roosts, where they will live on their own or in small groups.

Threats

Pipistrelle bats can live for up to 16 years in the wild, but most live to the age of 4 or 5. They have few natural predators because they are nocturnal, so they are hidden away from diurnal (daytime) predators. They can also escape from many predators through flight. The tawny owl is one of the few predators that can catch a pipistrelle bat in the air. Tawny owls can also catch bats that are resting in the open.

▼ Tawny owls are nocturnal predators. They swoop down silently on their prey, taking it by surprise.

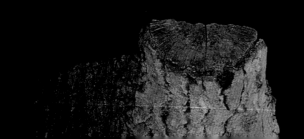

Severe weather conditions may cause a female bat to abandon her pup if she cannot find enough food to produce milk. This 1-week-old abandoned pup is being fed goat's milk in a bat hospital.

When bats wake from hibernation they are often very drowsy. It can take half an hour to raise their body temperature high enough to fly. This makes them very vulnerable to predators on the ground, especially cats.

Cold weather can be a great threat to nursing pipistrelle bats. Few insects fly in cold or wet weather, which reduces the amount of food available to nursing females. This may affect the amount of milk they can produce for their infants. Very hungry pups that crawl from the roost before they are ready to fly may fall and die. Since most pipistrelle bats only produce a single pup at a time, the mother would not be able to produce another pup until the following year.

SUPERSTITIONS

In the past, bats were associated with witches because they fly at night. They have also been linked with the vampire myth in which bats bite humans and suck their blood. However in China, bats are thought to bring good luck, especially if they enter your home.

People and bats

People are the pipistrelle's biggest threat. In the countryside, chemical pesticides used on crops kill millions of insects, which are the bat's prey. Insect populations are also reduced by new building developments, which destroy flowers, woodland and ponds. If bats cannot find enough insect food, they will starve.

Many of the bat's traditional roost sites, such as old hollow trees, have been cut down to make way for new buildings. Today, pipistrelle bats rely on houses and other buildings for roost sites. Here they can act as a natural form of pest control by eating midges, mosquitoes and woodworm beetles, which are a nuisance to people and buildings.

▼ Pesticides sprayed on crops can affect bats as well as their prey. Bats that eat insects sprayed with pesticides can be poisoned, too.

BAT BOXES

Bat boxes provide artificial roost sites, which help to replace natural sites lost through tree clearance. Instead of an entrance hole, bats enter the box through a gap at the bottom of the box which is 15–20 mm wide. The chamber inside holds many bats.

▲ By facing in different directions, these three bat boxes provide different temperature conditions for summer and winter.

Unfortunately, bats roosting in houses are threatened by disturbance due to building work, or harm from chemical treatments used to kill woodworm or preserve roof timbers. Although it is against the law in Britain and Europe to deliberately harm bats or disturb their roost sites, many people harm them accidentally because they do not realise they are living in their homes.

Bat Life Cycle

6 Female bats can mate when they are 1 year old. Male bats first mate when they are 2 years old.

1 A new-born bat is blind, furless and about 2 cm in length. Usually only one pup is born to each female.

2 The pup's eyes open when it is about 1 week old.

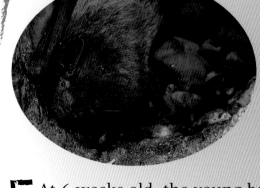

5 At 6 weeks old, the young bat leaves the nursery roost with its mother. Later it joins the winter roost, where it will hibernate.

4 The pup stays with its mother for a few weeks while it learns to hunt insects.

3 At 3 weeks old the pup is fully furred and will make its first flight.

28

Bat Clues

Look out for the following clues to help you find signs of a bat:

Roost holes
A dark-brown smudge may be visible around a well-used roost access hole. This is from the bat's body oils.

Dusk
A good time to see pipistrelle bats is when they are leaving the roost at dusk. They stream out of the roost one by one and fly around the entrance briefly before starting to hunt.

June–July
Bats are particularly active around their roost site in June or July, when young bats are learning to fly.

Calls
While many of the sounds that bats make are too high for humans' hearing range, social calls, especially those made when bats first leave the roost, can sometimes be heard as a 'chonk' sound. Special machines called bat detectors can be used to listen to bats' calls.

Droppings
Bat droppings are dark-brown or black in colour and cylindrical in shape. They crumble easily if they are old and dried out, and usually contain fragments of insects, such as wings and other body parts. Bat droppings may be found beneath the entrance to an active roost, on windowsills, stuck to walls, or on the ground.

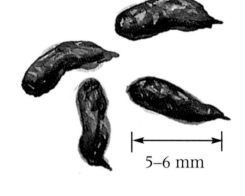

5–6 mm

Daytime
Occasionally, bats can be seen during the daytime. This is usually in winter, when they have left the hibernation roost to find food.

Footprints
Bat footprints are very rare. They are most likely to be found in soft mud near water. The back print is made by the five toes on each foot, while the front print is a small mark made by the thumb.

Thumb

Back print

Glossary

airborne Supported by the air.

colonies Groups of the same type of animals that live together.

domestic An animal that is bred as a pet or for food.

dusk The time just after sunset and before it gets dark at night.

echolocation A way of detecting objects by measuring the time it takes sounds to bounce off the objects and return as an echo.

forage To search for food.

habitat The area where an animal or plant naturally lives.

hibernate To enter a deep sleep that lasts most of the winter.

hibernation roost A roost used by bats to hibernate during the winter.

insectivore An animal that eats mainly insects.

lagoon A small body of water connected to the sea.

mammal A warm-blooded animal that produces live young. Rats, cats and people are mammals.

marine To do with the sea, for example, an animal that lives in the sea.

maternity colony A group of female bats raising young together.

nocturnal A animal that is active at night.

nursery roost A roost used by female bats to raise their young.

pesticides Chemicals that are used to kill pests such as insects.

population The number of bats that live in one place.

predator An animal that kills and eats other animals.

prey Animals that are killed and eaten by predators.

pup A young bat. Young dogs, seals and rats are also called pups.

roosts Places where bats gather to rest or sleep.

species A group of animals that share the same features.

suckle To feed young from teats.

territorial To defend and control an area.

vegetation Various different plants that grow together forming a covering on the ground.

weaned Used to eating solid food rather than a mother's milk.

wingspan The distance between the wingtips of a flying animal.

Finding Out More

Other books to read

Animal Young: Mammals by Rod Theodorou (Heinemann, 2000)

Bizarre Beasts by Beatrice Fontanel (Wayland, 2000)

Classification: Animal Kingdom by Kate Whyman (Wayland, 2000)

Classifying Living Things: Classifying Mammals by Andrew Solway (Heinemann, 2003)

Illustrated Encyclopedia of Animals by Fran Pickering (Chrysalis, 2003)

Life Cycles: Cats and Other Mammals by Sally Morgan (Chrysalis, 2003)

Living Nature: Mammals by Angela Royston (Chrysalis, 2004)

The Wayland Book of Common British Mammals by Shirley Thompson (Wayland, 2000)

Weird Wildlife: Mammals by Jen Green (Raintree, 2003)

What's the Difference?: Mammals by Stephen Savage (Wayland, 2002)

Wild Britain: Towns & Cities by R. & L. Spilsbury (Heinemann, 2003)

Learning About Life Cycles: The Life Cycle of a Bean, Cat, Chicken, Frog, Honeybee and Salmon All by Ruth Thomson (Wayland, 2006 & 2007)

Organisations to contact

The Bat Conservation Trust
15 Cloisters House, 8 Battersea Park Road, London SW8 4BG
www.bats.org.uk
An organisation devoted to the conservation of bats and their habitats in the British Isles, with a helpline and a Young Batworker's Club.

Countryside Foundation for Education
PO Box 8, Hebden Bridge HX7 5YJ
www.countrysidefoundation.org.uk
An organisation that produces training and teaching materials to help the understanding of the countryside and its problems.

English Nature
Northminster House, Peterborough, Cambridgeshire PE1 1UA
www.english-nature.org.uk
A government body that promotes the conservation of English wildlife and the natural environment.

The Mammal Society
2B Inworth Street, London SW11 3EP
www.abdn.ac.uk/mammal/
This organisation promotes the study and conservation of British mammals.

Wildlife Watch
National Office, The Kiln, Waterside, Mather Road, Newark NG24 1WT
www.wildlifetrusts.org
The junior branch of the Wildlife Trusts, a network of local wildlife trusts that care for nature reserves and protect a huge number of habitats and species.

Index

Page numbers in **bold** refer to a photograph or illustration.